ANIMA
Resuscitation

A Brown American Girl's Spiritual Poetic Journey Through Social Injustice, Forced Vaccination, and Feminine Uprising Amid the COVID-19 Pandemic

DIANA S. RICE

© 2024 by Diana S. Rice

All rights reserved. No part of this publication may be reproduced, distributed, or transmitted in any form or by any means, including photocopying, recording, or other electronic or mechanical methods, without the prior written permission of the author, except in the case of brief quotations embodied in critical reviews and certain other noncommercial uses permitted by copyright law. For permission requests, email the author at the address: info@dianasrice.com

First Edition

ISBN: [ISBN Number]

Published by Firebrand Publishing

Printed in United States of America.

Illustrations by Diana S. Rice

POEMS

OXYGEN	6
Preface	7
Be the Oxygen	9
Dismantling	13
The Last Supper	17
Police Line Do Not Cross	23
Whistlin' Dixie	27
Where is Her Torch?	31
Bible Belt	35
Un\/🪓D	38
Preface	39
Doctor	41
Figuring Out Fauci	45
Pharmakeia	49

Oh, Yeaaah!	53
Communal Conundrum Odyssey	57
5G Conspiracist	61
Píldora Roja de Rona	65
Florida Woman	69
FEMINISTA	72
Preface	73
Why I Shaved Thy Head (5 Haikus)	75
Are You Ok?	77
Femininity Cocoon	81
Anima Resuscitation	85

OXYGEN IN 2020

I dedicate the following poems

To the beautiful chocolate, cinnamon,

and caramel souls who have come across my path

To those who let me in and allowed me to laugh

To the black boys who have always had my back

To the police who feel they are under attack

To those who call themselves Christians and live in the south

To those who have told me to shut my mouth

To my family and friends

To all the ones who understand

PREFACE

In March 2020, as the COVID-19 pandemic forced us all into lockdown, America erupted in protest following the murder of George Floyd by a white police officer. The resulting outrage was driven by a long history of racial injustices in the country, which had seen black and brown people, disproportionately affected and marginalized. As a brown Latina woman working as a Licensed Mental Health Counselor in an alternative high school in Broward County, I bore witness to how these events impacted the young black and brown individuals with whom I worked. Already struggling with lockdown in toxic homes and the mental health challenges this presented, my clients found their anxiety and depression considerably worsened by the steady drip of distressing news from the wider world. My own experiences of racism, which saw me jailed for one night in 1992, continue to haunt me, and when I saw how the world was responding to this new crisis, I knew I needed to find an outlet for my emotions. And so, I turned to my digital art and poetry as a way of processing the tumultuous events of 2020, and the Oxygen collection is the result. This personal collection of work helped me to find a way of expressing my own experiences of racism and racial injustice and offers a way for readers to explore their own feelings and engage in some of the difficult conversations that our society must confront if we hope to achieve lasting change.

BE THE OXYGEN

Tue, Jun 2, 2020, 8:41 AM

The statement that describes 2020.

I can't breathe!

Rising up the fears of many.

I can't breathe!

Bringing forth our secret thoughts.

I can't breathe!

As the world is being torn apart.

I can't breathe!

Suicides rocked my community.

I can't breathe!

There is no political immunity.

I can't breathe!

Pestilence that took over the world.

I can't breathe!

Police brutality towards black boys & girls.

I can't breathe!

Black lives do matter.

I can't breathe!

Racism needs to be shattered.

I can't breathe!

Wake up and look within.

I can't breathe!

Please deal with YOUR sin.

I can't breathe!

God's bringing to light the heart of each man.

I can't breathe!

Waking up our souls, so we understand.

I can't breathe!

From pestilence to great injustices.

I can't breathe!

We need to deal with all the corruption.

For those who say that ALL lives matter.

Yes, of course, but we're trying to shatter.

Inequality started long ago.

Created an unfair status quo.

So please stop being so defensive.

Take off your privilege lenses.

Take a deep breath because you can.

Take a minute to understand.

They can't breathe! We can't breathe!

Be the oxygen for others.

Take care of our brown & black sisters and brothers.

DISMANTLING

Fri, Jun 19, 2020, 11:45 AM

Black lives matter.
All lives matter.
Black lives matter.
All lives matter.

What about the blue?
What about me?
What about you?

What about realizing it's all about sin.
Stop pointing fingers and start looking within.
A world of injustice from the beginning of time.
Human nature-loving power is the start of the crime.

2020 is a year of real heart exposure.
Ending a race war, looking for closure.

Dismantling of the red, the white, and the blue. A HIS story of greed we wish was not true.

Was taught it was due to freedom of religion. As white man decided to make all the decisions.

A country raped in the name of equality. My heartbroken longing to see.

Truly!

> "We hold these truths to be self-evident that all men are created equal, that they are endowed by their Creator with certain unalienable Rights, that among these are Life, Liberty, and the Pursuit of Happiness."
>
> -Declaration of Independence, July 4th, 1776

Life, liberty, and the pursuit of happiness. Galatians 3:28 help me focus on oneness.

My brown flesh at battle with my spirit.
The Holy Spirit speaking, please Jesus,
help me hear it!

Black lives matter.

All lives matter.

Black lives matter.

All lives matter.

What about the blue?

What about me?

What about you?

The Last Supper

Tue, Jun 23, 2020, 5:30 PM

Is Christianity under attack?

Because a statue that represents your faith needs to fall?

Where in the Bible does it say to create statutes to represent God?

To bow down to a manmade call.

Idols forefathers put in place to ease the guilt of dehumanizing others.

Politically activated into race for the prideful oppression of sisters and brothers.

Age of hypocrisy.

Age of apostasy.

Age of technological velocity.

2020!

As we hunger and thirst for truth.
In a world of fake news.

Capitalism.

Marxism.

Communism.

Socialism.

Racism.

Sexism.

Every Ism Satan uses.

To steal.

To kill.

To destroy.

Buying into the separation to save our money and power.

Being rewarded for the wicked ways of greed while being coy.

Acting shy, hiding behind religion and politics in order to save our wealth.

The wealth that will turn to moths and rust.

While our bodies turn to dust.

Christian!

Does it bother you to tear down a European representative of our Savior?

Why?

Do you feel that we are under attack?

Cry!

Cry out to the Jesus you claim to follow.

Instead of feeling attacked, maybe it's the God of the Bible, you say you believe in.

Dealing with sin.

Within!

Allowing us all to be sifted.

To be refined.

I know it's hard to swallow.

Christian! We are being defined!

Open up that Bible.

The bread of life.
The living water.

The last supper.

Repent!

POLICE LINE DO NOT CROSS

Wed. Jun 24, 2020, 3:48 PM

How many times has this line been crossed?
How many times does a case get tossed?

Out of court.
Fallen short.

The blue.
Taking you.

Pass the line.

How many times do we need to hear?
How many moms have to live in fear?

Your hoodie.

Becomes your jury.

The blue.

Mistaking you.

Pass the line.

How many times we've seen them instigate?

How many times have we seen them terminate?

Black and brown.

Keep them down.

The blue.

Killing you.

Pass the line.

Police line do not cross.

Police line do not cross.

Bad apples are being tossed.

Bad apples are being tossed.

As America finally is waking up to the rotten smell!

The ringing of screams through the crack of the liberty bell!

A song of patriotism.

For the blue.

How long before they will protect you?

WHISTLIN' DIXIE

Fri. Jun 26, 2020, 2:36 PM

A short leash was placed on chocolate souls.
Tricked by vanilla elites whistlin' dixie.
Claiming all men are created equal.
Conveniently forgetting about the prequel.

A symbol that waves blatantly in the wind
of oppression.

Excuses are being made by a culture of pride.
A song of the south will rise again.
But you say we are your friend.

Are we?

Then let loose of the noose that divides!

North and South.

Divided we fall, there are no sides!

Are there?

Vanilla and chocolate swirl, yum, my favorite!
While I eat a sugar cone of hope with a new tune.
Praying and swaying as I watch ropes fall down.
In hopes of a new sound.

Look away!

Look away!

Look away!

Dixie Land.

Where is Her Torch?

Fri, Jun 26, 2020, 5:06 PM

Politicians have become magicians in the land of the free.

While a statue too big to come down goes by Lady Liberty.

Where is your torch that is supposed to light the way?

Is it drowning in the tears of shame?

Swirling into an abyss of politics.

Floating far away.

While we suffocate each other six feet apart at the magic show, created by the news.

Making sure each one is heard on social platforms, our essential point of view.

Democrat or Republican.

Do you really think Trump or Biden?

No man will save us but the Prince of Peace. 2020 is the year when the 4th of July will cease.

Vote red.

Vote blue.

It won't save you!

As we swim alongside her torch of enlightenment.

Praying that we don't drown!

BIBLE BELT
Fri, Jun 26, 2020, 9:16 PM

I'm still trying to wrap my mind around those who call themselves Christian while creating hate in their heart in the name of history, culture, and pride.

Dust off that Bible and read what's inside.

Doesn't the Living Word say,
"Love your enemy" &
"Pride comes before the fall"?

Will you actually answer His call?

Numerous times I've been to your churches with potluck dinners of saturated fats and high fructose corn syrup, while obesity is killing the children.

Crack open that Bible to see who is the villain.

Doesn't the Living Word say,
"Don't exasperate your children" &
"Your body is a temple"?

Are you living by example?

Sunday, we worship God under a roof
of segregation then go home to enjoy a
sport of integrated mutilation.

Bonding through sensations,
as we call it integration.

Trying to raise kids by
checking off boxes,
creating habits.

Wolves in sheep's clothing!

As little kids of color are groaning.

Through the deep roots of the plantation owner his-story, hanging on tight to a Christianity I don't find in the Bible.

It's time to let go of the title.

We are all liable.

USA!

One nation under God, huh?

Time to choose which one...

UnVD

I dedicate the following poems

To those who were coerced against their will

To those who have swallowed the big red pill

To the brave truckers who fought for our freedom

To Big Pharma, who has poisoned the children

To global elitists who think they are in control

To Jesus who is my savior and Lord

To my family and friends

To all the ones who understand

PREFACE

This collection of poetry is an outpouring of my innermost feelings and thoughts regarding the handling of the COVID-19 pandemic by science and mainstream media. As a lover of science, the lack of double-blind studies and control groups in the research presented to the public troubled me deeply. As someone who always questioned scientific findings, I was disheartened by the fear and censorship surrounding the questioning of the pandemic's handling. My experience working in the mental health field brought to light the harmful effects of pharmaceuticals on young people and left me with growing concerns about the repercussions of the vaccine mandates. My background in women's studies reinforced the importance of individual rights and freedoms, including the right to make decisions about our bodies. However, the increasing gaslighting from those around me and the constant barrage of fear-inducing content on social media made maintaining my sense of clarity and focus a challenge. Despite my efforts to exercise my legal right to reasonable accommodations, my employer mandated that I receive the COVID-19 vaccine, resulting in my termination. This experience was incredibly difficult, and this collection of poetry represents my grappling with the complex emotions and challenges that arose during that time.

Doctor

Sun, Jan 9, 2022, 3:46 PM

Doctor
Physician
Why are you blinded from nutrition?

For the slithering greed of Big Pharma
has clipped your wings!

No longer can you fly.

Doctor
Physician
Are you a medical practitioner?

For the slithering seed of Big Pharma
has brainwashed you into believing their lie!

No longer can you sing.

Doctor
Physician
This western tradition

Diagnosing

Medicating

Keeping us focused on the hocus pocus as we lose our locus...

Locus of control!

Return to the Hippocratic oath of first do no harm.

Disarm!

Disarm the witchcraft and dark forces that keep us tethered to a billion-dollar machine!

Creating illnesses in labs overseas as they come to our rescue with their dreams.

The nightmare of greed...

Doctor
Physician
Make the decision.

To take back your power of healing.

Let your wings soar like an eagle
in the land of the free.

Be the angel you were meant to be...

Wondering why the great upheaval?
For the love of money is the root of all
kinds of evil!

Figuring Out Fauci

Thu, Feb 10, 2022, 3:00 PM

A man I never heard of until March of 2020.
A father figure amid the pandemic frenzy.
It seemed like he knew medical science plenty.
But his promises kept coming up empty.

After I questioned his cronies, "follow the science."

As a conspiracy theorist forced into compliance.

I am praying to God to give me intuitive guidance.

Then they MANDATED me to carry an immunized license.

Wait, what? Are you taking my medical freedom?

When did my relationship with my doc become a threesome?

Fired from my job as I stood for my rights, so lonesome!

Shame and guilt from mob bosses,
so gruesome!

Follow the science.
Follow the science.
I did, and it led me to your bias.
Oh yeah, I followed the science.
Led me straight to your cash allowance.

As I kept searching for the other scientific truth.
I was straightening my tinfoil hat while becoming a freedom sleuth.

The global elitist are trying to pull out
my wisdom tooth.

You are forcing your way into the bodies
of unprotected youth.

When was the last time you saw actual patients?
Instead of hanging around mainstream media
stations, Or hanging with nefarious characters
pushing medications.
While you pulled the string of fear in our nation.

The cult you created for years runs deep.
While so many in dread are frozen asleep.
As truckers are honking, waking up the sheep.
While the children continue to weep.

Follow the science.
Follow the science.
I did, and it led me to your bias.
Oh yeah, I followed the science.
Led me straight to your payout alliance.

Yo! Fauci! I'm unto your great upheaval.
Because I know the love of money is the root
of all kinds of evil!

Pharmakeia

Sun, Jan 9, 2022, 5:20 PM

Pharmakeia, the root word of pharmaceutical, means magic, sorcery, and witchcraft, often found in connection with idolatry in the Bible.

But who is liable?

Have you ever wondered why the symbol is two snakes slithering up to wings?

Let's get to the root of your poisoning.

They are brainwashing with continual moistening.

Through Big Tech's constant loitering.

You are canceling anyone who questions your so-called science!

Building an alliance.

Sorcerers are casting the giant spell.

Demons straight from the pit of hell.

While pretending to wish us well.

As children are led like sacrificial lambs to the altar.

Just to be slaughtered!

Fear porn creates mass formation psychosis, a power monopoly of segregation.

Warlocks in white coats of deception.

Wolves in sheep's clothing of perception.

Totalitarians are banking on these injections.

"Follow the science."

HA!

NO!!....

Follow the money.

You are lining your pockets with this great upheaval.

For the love of money is the root
of all kinds of evil!

OH, YEAAAH!

Mon. Jan 24, 2022, 11:12 AM

Reckless devotion into mass formation psychosis.

We are allowing the media to be confirmation bias voices.

Souls with free-floating anxiety in mandated isolation.

They are allowing forced fear to be the consolation.

Oh yeah!

Here comes Kool-Aid.

Here comes Kool-Aid.

He's going to save da day!

Here comes Kool-Aid.

Here comes Kool-Aid.

He's going to chase your fears away.

What has happened to the beauty of science?

Double-blind studies, no comorbidities, control groups, no bias?

Years of research with brilliant intellects.

Down the drain as big tech and mainstream media misdirects.

Oh yeah!

Here comes Kool-Aid.

Here comes Kool-Aid.

He's going to save da day!

Here comes Kool-Aid.

Here comes Kool-Aid.

He's going to chase your tears away.

Population control.

Survival of the fittest.

Top 1 percent on a roll.

Have I passed your conquest?

Oh yeah!

Here comes Kool-Aid.

Here comes Kool-Aid.

He's going to save da day!

Here comes Kool-Aid.

Here comes Kool-Aid.

He's going to chase your jeers away.

Please don't tread on me.

I am American.

Land of the FREE!

A Good Samaritan.

Are you drunk yet from this great upheaval?

Remember, the love of money
is the root of all kinds of evil.

Communal Conundrum Odyssey

Tue, Feb 1, 2022, 5:38 PM

Be aware that your soul is being sold as you blindly fall into the wormhole created by greed.

Tracking your every move as you continue to groove through the trail of this narcissistic seed.

Secretly planted on your connection journey as you eagerly wait on the red notification to get you high.

Always wondering why.

Why doesn't anyone like my stuff?
Am I not enough?

Two hours go by in this matrix of forced-fed info from artificial intelligence.

While Big Pharma, Big Government, and Big Tech hide the evidence.

Thinking you are weak in the mind.

But Jesus, you remind.

You remind my soul.
This is the goal.

The battle is real, and we must stay focused on the Living Word inspired.

This is the spiritual war waging, and You prepare us for the slithering liar.

The liar who taunts us through airwaves. As we isolate in our caves.

We want to be socially connected but too anxious or depressed as we grieve what once was.

This is the age of apostasy.
We are falling into ecstasy.

I am hoping to become an influencer for You!

As I strap on the helmet of salvation while grabbing your pierced hand to lift me out of this matrix of insanity.

Let me focus on the trail that leads to everlasting instead of the pressures of this vanity.

The social dilemma of this great upheaval.

For the love of money is the root of all kinds of evil.

5G Conspiracist

Tue, Feb 1, 2022, 6:03 PM

CDC, FDA deny 5G health risks.
As I'm deemed an uneducated tinfoil hat conspiracist.

Big government elitists.
Mandating us to be realists.

But real to who?
To me, to you?

Those that work hard and try to do the right thing.

While they take our money as a sacrificial offering.

Turning the land of the wild and free,
Into whatever the billionaires want it to be.

While we melt with radiation.
Believing their interpretation.

Of a trillion-dollar sick care system.
As bad actors suck up all of our wisdom.

When has the government ever really cared?

The duopoly of millionaires get their thousand-dollar haircuts, fly their private jets, wear designer dresses to private galas using our hopes to line their pockets.

All are pretending to care about us!

I'm not a white supremacist.
Nor a Republican or a Democrat.

Just a soul who wears a tinfoil hat!

An intelligent brain who questions the mainstream narrative.
A loving spirit examining the fake dream negative.

In a land taken from Native Americans and built on the backs of enslaved Africans while thousands of soldiers with PTSD are rolling in their graves.

Rise up!
Wake up!

Swallow your big red pill.

The entire political swamp needs to be
removed from the hill.

Before more beautiful souls jump sixty
stories
in pain.
And our children and teens keep going
insane.

We are in a matrix of truth revealed,

Waiting for the Bible's seven seals.
To be broken.

Ah yes, another mythical conspiracy.
In the heart of this bureaucratic hypocrisy.

I will continue to pray, focus, heal and follow Christ.

Straightening my tin foil hat and will
continue
to be nice.

As I ask for protection from this great
upheaval.

For the love of money is the root of all
kinds of evil!

Píldora Roja de Rona

Mon. Feb 21, 2022, 5:05 PM

I was living life normally in the month of March. In the 2020th year of our Lord.

The media began murmuring of a pestilence. As they were reciting in one hypnotic accord.

A virus is spreading throughout the nations.
No stopping this manifestation.
Was it man-made or its own creation?
We were glued to every mainstream news station.

Coronavirus disease 2019!

It's coming for me.
It's coming for you.
Oh no! What are we going to do?
We're all going to die of the Wuhan flu.

We were clinging on tight to our loved ones.
Free-falling into the abyss of insanity.

The media began whispering lockdown estimates. As they coerced with lies from big pharmacy.

A virus has spread throughout the nations.
We can stop this manifestation.
With a manufactured quick studied creation.
They were screaming from every media station.

Coronavirus disease 2019!

It's coming for me.
It's coming for you.
Oh no! What are we going to do?
We all need inoculation of the Wuhan flu.

Slowly stepping outside of our homes.
Making sure we have on our masks.
The media began bullying the unvaccinated.
As the scared kept sipping on their flask.

A virus has spread throughout the nations.
We can't stop this manifestation.

Too many new variant creations.
The fear tactics of every news station.

Coronavirus disease 2019!

It's coming for me.
It's coming for you.
Oh no! What are we going to do?

Booster.
Rooster.
Keep trying to seduce her.
With their cock a doodle doo....

WAKE UP, FOOL!

They don't care about you!

A virus has spread throughout the nations.
We can stop this manifestation.
Critically think and look at the entire equation.
See who pays these legacy news stations.

Peacefully I understand this great upheaval.

For the love of money is the root of all kinds of evil!

Florida Woman

Pandemic atrocities.

Forced velocities.

This hurricane of insane monstrosities.

Hurricane CoVid19.

A category 5 trying to take on this Florida woman.

Giving her strength as she fought for the humans.

I thought I was raised in the land of the free because of the brave.

Then the swamp of Washington D.C. began to cave.

Cave under lust of the power pressure.
Giving up the true treasure.

The treasure of all of our freedom.
Kept seeing the evil demons.

Of greed!
Of power!

I said no all the way to the last hour.
Then I was fired!

Many people like to yell, my body, my choice to kill a baby!
Then had the audacity to take away my voice and gaslit me to make me look crazy.

Like I was some mass murderer who wanted to kill everybody's grandparents

High emotions blinding not seeing these elitists weren't being transparent.

Fear porn rush

Drowning us

In waves of depression and anxiety.

Losing our humanity!

Listen I am not a Republican or a Democrat.

But I am grateful that DeSantis and Ladapo had my back.

When other states totally neglected how to be human.

Never thought I would be this appreciative to be a Florida woman!

This American understood how this was so illegal.

For the love of money is the root of all kinds of evil!

FEMINISTA

I dedicate the following poems

To Jesus the first feminist

To those who are misogynist

To the many who fought for women's rights

To those who spend hours crying at night

To the souls who just want equality

To those who are stuck and cannot speak

To my family and friends

To all the ones who understand

On a warm September day in 2022, while my husband was away traveling, a stirring in the depths of my soul overwhelmed me. The need for a radical change was palpable, a need to break free from the expectations and constraints of society. With courage pulsing through my veins, i grabbed my scissors and slowly cut away my long, luscious locks.

As you delve into this collection of poetry, you may find yourself wondering what possessed a 50-year-old woman to make such a drastic decision. Perhaps my motives were rooted in my desire to shed the weight of societal expectations or to take a stand against the limitations placed upon us as women. Or maybe, as a nod to sinead o'connor, i sought to boldly reclaim my identity and speak my truth by baring my bald head to the world.

Whatever the reason, this collection is a manifestation of my deepest emotions and reflections during that period of metamorphosis. Through my words and imagery, i invite you to join me on a journey of self-discovery and exploration - a journey that is both deeply personal and universally relevant. By the end of these pages, i hope that you will have unraveled my secret, understood my transformative experience, and found inspiration in your own path to self-realization.

Why I Shaved My Head (5 Haikus)

Wed, Sep 21, 2022, 8:43 AM

Lamenting our sin
Transgression to divine law
Expressing battle

    Rebel against man
    Pressure to be feminine
    Patriarchy rule

        Challenge social quo
        To know who truly loves me
        Beauty is within

            Chemical freedom
            Independence of heat tools
            Saving my money

                A form of cutting
                Feeling the pain for others
                Spiritual breakthrough

Are You Ok?

Fri. Sep 23, 2022, 5:56 AM

Female buzz cut sparks the question.
Faces of concern.
Assumptions of illness.
Eyes are wide as I continue to learn.

Genuine care?
Curiosity?
Did I disturb your insides?

Good!

Thank you for asking, Am I Ok?

It does mean a lot to me that you care,

But,

This is what I really want to share,

It's 2022.

Is anybody Ok?!

Are you?
NO, REALLY, ARE YOU?!

Turn on the news.
Talk to a teacher.
USA is crumbling.
Pride of the preacher.

Tik Tokked teens.
Family dying.
Humans are brewing.
Flashbacks keep flying.

How is it that after fifty years of roaming this earth I have not been desensitized?

Is it a mental illness?

Did I have a Brittany moment?

Or was it a supernatural experience turning me into GI Jane?

A phoenix rising?

Am I going insane?

Those who know me for a long time ain't surprised.

I mean some want me medicated.

I get it.

A walking paradox that many can't figure out, so they just say I'm crazy.

Ahh, the myth of normal!

But am I OK?

No, but Yes, I say.

Explain my decision politely to not complicate your stay.

"Thank you for caring"
then cordially walk away...

Femininity Cocoon

Sun, Oct 23, 2022, 3:50 PM

A second puberty of the feminine.
Punished by a society of gentlemen.
Staying skinny as a skeleton.
As we continue losing estrogen.

Westernization of the womanizer.
Believing the lying advertiser.
In the palm of the colonizer.
While we become the equalizer.

Urging!
Purging!

Fighting to be securely respected.
While our parts are being dissected.
Little girls are disgustingly subjected.
Pornography and trafficking infected.

Five decades of the feminine road.
Trying to figure out the Biblical code.
Cocooned in Jesus's episode.
As we deal with the overload.

Surging!
Emerging!

On a road of soulful dreams.
Where menopause is esteemed.
Where periods are not unclean.
Not our body, but brains are seen.

Chrysalis becoming deeper.
Transform us into new creatures.
Silencing the oppressive preachers.
Wings drying to fly as radiant teachers.

Daughters of the King!

Merging!
Disturbing!

The status quo.

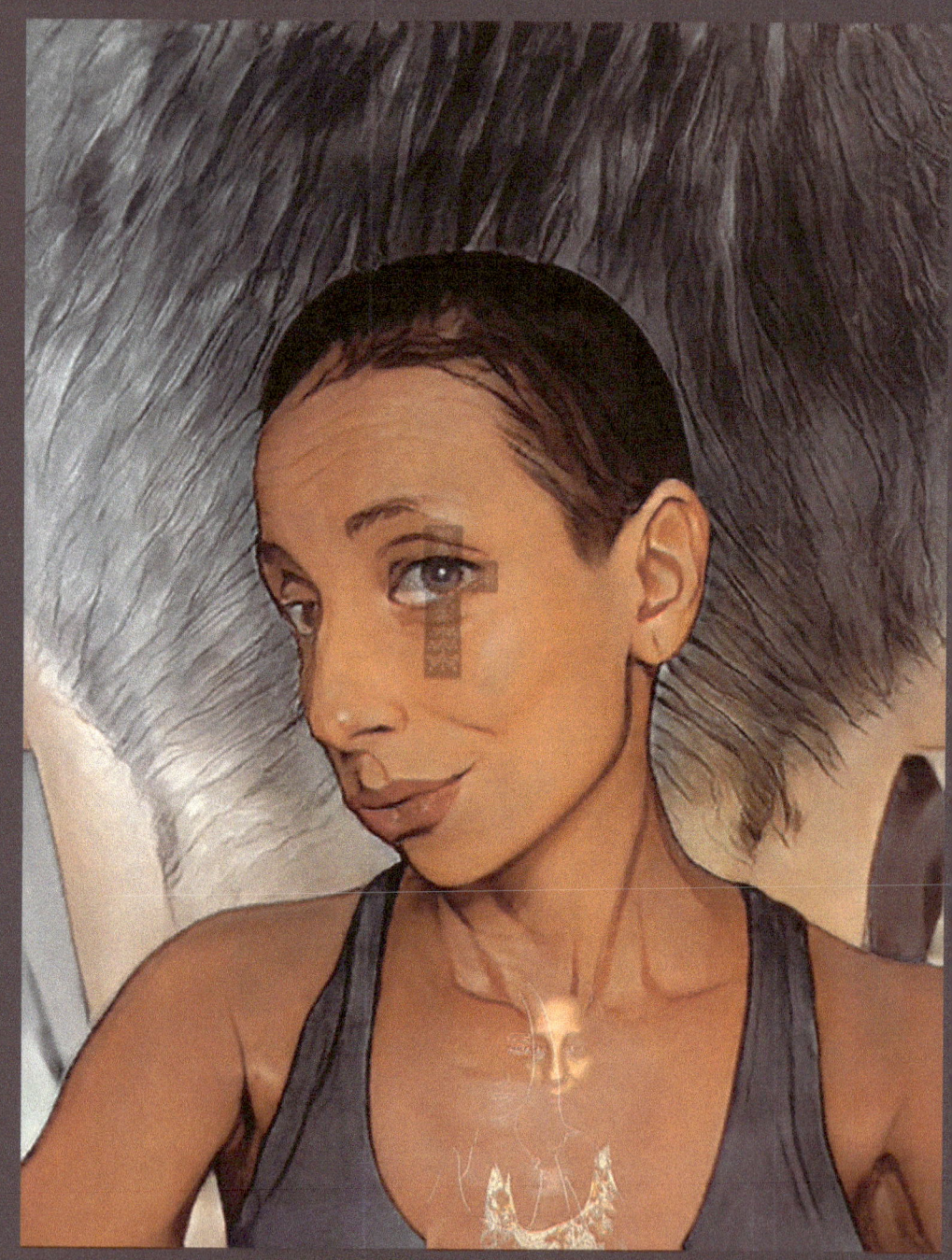

Anima Resuscitation

Tue. Nov 1, 2022, 3:41 PM

Heart beating (boom, boom, boom)

Thoughts fleeting (zoom, zoom, zoom)

As I remember the pope's picture being ripped on national TV in 1992

This brave feminine beauty risked everything for what she believed was true

Bald head

She knew

She knew

Scissors to head slowly cutting

Relief from feeling nothing

Strands of female fronting

Free from sexual hunting

Deep spiritual touching

Awakening soul becoming

Heart beating (thump, thump, thump)

Thoughts fleeting (bump, bump, bump)

Looking into the mirror at a distant known stranger

Wondering who she is and whether she was in danger

Bald head

I knew

I knew

Walking through salvation

Angry at corporations

Fighting the inoculation

Spirit war in the hesitation

Not wanting this obligation

Peace in the liberation

Anima resuscitation

www.ingramcontent.com/pod-product-compliance
Lightning Source LLC
Chambersburg PA
CBHW061804070526
44586CB00023B/2703